MOTHERS

Boyd K. Packer
with illustrations by the author

Deseret Book Company
Salt Lake City, Utah

Second printing 1999 by Deseret Book Company.

ISBN 0-87747-650-0

Printed in the United States of America   71976-6465
10   9   8   7   6   5   4   3   2

Sometimes when I have a few private moments (and they are few) I try to express myself in painting. When invited to prepare a tribute to mothers and to illustrate it, I thought of a painting by Jean-Francois Millet, a Frenchman who lived from 1814 to 1875. He is best known for his paintings *The Gleaners* and *The Angelus*. Another of his works—not well known—has always impressed me. Entitled *Feeding Her Little Birds*, it depicts a peasant mother spooning food to her children, and captures a tender picture of motherhood in the nourishing of little ones. This painting, sometimes also called *Feeding Her Nestlings*, hangs in the museum in Lille, France, and sets the theme for the illustrations in this booklet.

*M*y mother often told us of her childhood. Her mother died in a typhoid epidemic when she was six, and she went to live in a little farming community with her grandmother. Her fondest childhood memories recalled the summer evenings when she wandered alone along the banks of the river and through the fields, listening to the birds. She loved the call of the mourning doves. All her life she expressed her joy at God's creations. All her children inherited a love of nature from her.

We now live in a wooded area where there are many birds, and I often think of Mother when I see a brood of nestlings. How instinctively a mother bird looks after her brood and feeds them. How anxiously she teaches them to fly and to fend for themselves. How fearlessly she flies to their protection.

This God-given instinct of motherhood is common in all of God's creations. It is natural and it is good.

Never has there been a time when it is more important to encourage and protect the ideals of motherhood. Never across the earth has there been more said about women, about womanhood, about motherhood. So much talk—and so much of it misguided.

They talk about a woman's sphere,
As though it has a limit;

There's not a place in earth or heaven,
There's not a task to mankind given,

There's not a blessing nor a woe,
There's not a whispered yes or no,

There's not a life, or death, or birth,
That has a feather's weight of worth . . .

Without a woman in it.
(Anon.)

There is so much to be lost if the ideals of womanhood and of motherhood are tampered with or tarnished.

When I speak of mothers, I speak not only of those women who have borne children, but also of those who have fostered children born to others, and of the many women who, without children of their own, have mothered the children of others.

The bearing of children is but the beginning—a few months and it is finished. Fostering and molding a child's character is never done. It takes a lifetime and more.

There are sisters who have assumed the role of mother for younger brothers and sisters. Other wonderful women have fostered the welfare of youngsters because the youngsters needed that influence and

8

because those women needed someone to "do for." Their influence has been that of a mother, both as to the effect on those children and as it fostered the instinctive virtues of motherhood.

The sensitivity of a mother. There are natural attributes that a woman possesses that are polished to a fine and useful capacity by motherhood. Some of these things men cannot do very well. There are some instinctive, sensitive things that a woman will *feel* when a man cannot *see* them. Some of them are spiritual things.

President David O. McKay taught this to the General Authorities one day in the temple when he said, "Brethren, you must take time to meditate."

Then he told us of an experience of one of the past General Authorities. His son worked on a railroad that went up Emigration Canyon to the mines east of Salt Lake City a number of years ago. This young man, who was working as a switchman, was found crushed to death under the train. His mother had the feeling that someone had pushed him under the train and had taken his life, so when the funeral services were held, she was not comforted.

After she had been mourning for some weeks, the young man appeared to her. He said, "Mother, I've been trying to get to Father to tell him it was just an accident. I had thrown the switch and was running to catch on to the handlebars, but my foot tripped against a root at the side of the rail, and I was thrown under the train. It really was an accident. I've been trying to get to Father, but he's too busy at the office. I can't reach him." The son then told his mother that he was happy, and she was greatly consoled.

It was the statement, "I've been trying to get to Father . . . I can't reach him," that concerned President McKay. "Don't become so busy at the office that spiritual forces are not able to reach you," he counseled.

Men may miss many things that are spiritual. Women somehow instinctively make time for these things. It is that sensitivity that is refined by motherhood. Should that be tampered with, or put aside, or smothered? Oh, how great the loss! Never were we more in need of those tender virtues than today.

Women are deeply sensitive spiritually. How tragic it would be to pull them into a man's world. Oh, what a loss! How tragic if a woman by decision avoids motherhood, resents it, becomes a part-time mother, or, sadder yet, forsakes it.

The courage of a mother. Because women are sensitive, feminine, and tender and need protection does not mean that they may not be strong, even heroic.

In South Royalton, Vermont, in the village square, just a mile or two down the hill from the place where Joseph Smith was born, is a monument with an inscription to a Mrs. Handy, a heroine indeed.

On October 17, 1780, Robert Havens, a distant neighbor to Mrs. Handy, left his house in the wee

hours of the morning and ascended the hill behind the house to check on the sheep. He had been awakened by the barking of a neighbor's dog and feared that something was molesting the sheep. The boys had neglected to bring them in the night before. He found the animals safe. Then he looked back at his cabin as the first light of dawn passed over it. He stood pensively, sensing that something was wrong. Then he saw a large party of Indians move from the woods toward his cabin.

It was the time of the American Revolution. A large force of Indians, 300 in number, had been offered a bounty by the British—eight dollars a head for men, something less for boys, if they were alive. There was a lesser bounty for scalps.

This force, commanded by a Captain Haughton, moved down the river from cabin to cabin, capturing the men they could, killing those who resisted, and, with questionable humanity, leaving the women subjected to something less than death.

Some distance downstream the Handy family was warned. The father sent his wife and their two little youngsters toward the woods to hide. Then he set out on foot to warn others and to get help.

Mrs. Handy, with her son, age seven, and her baby daughter, climbed the hill toward the safety of the woods. As she reached the edge of the forest, a band of Indians stepped from the shadows. They took her little boy from her. She asked an Indian who spoke English what they intended to do with him.

12

She was told that they would take him to Canada and make a soldier of him.

As the Indian carried her sobbing son away, she made her way toward the river. Her little girl was screaming in panic and fear, pleading with her mother to keep the Indians away. The obvious course was to move downstream to the larger settlements, where there would be protection, but she did not do the obvious.

Instead, she found the English leader of the Indians and asked him what they intended to do with the little boys they had taken captive. She knew the boys couldn't endure the long march to Montreal, and she told him so. Her worst fears were then confirmed; if the boys couldn't endure the march, they would be killed.

This mother, with uncommon resolution, determined that they would not have her son. She turned back up the river to the bank opposite the place where they were gathering their captives. Somehow she managed to cross the river, assisted by an Indian who pulled her and her little girl ashore.

Oblivious to danger, she demanded the return of her son. The leader of the Indians, Captain Haughton, said that he could not control them; that it was none of his concern what they did.

"You are the commander here, and they must obey you," she said. Then, quoting scripture, she charged him that if innocent blood were shed, it would be on his head. "When the secrets of men's hearts are made known, you shall stand convicted," she warned him.

When her little boy was brought in to the camp, she took him by the hand and refused to let go. The Indians threatened her with knives and tomahawks. She defiantly replied that she would follow them every step of the way to Canada. She would never relent! They would not have her son!

Finally, in exasperation, they gave her permission to leave camp with her little fellow. She had proceeded but a few yards when she was captured again. This time the captain said, "You must stay. If the Indians catch you again, we'll never be able to persuade them to let you go. You'll have to wait in camp until the march north begins."

Other little boys were brought in. They clung to her in pathetic desperation. Somehow this twenty-seven-year-old mother with uncommon courage interceded for them as vigorously as she had for her own son.

When the assembled captives finally began the long march to Canada, Mrs. Handy crossed the river with her baby daughter and nine small boys—her son Michael, Roswell Parker, Andrew and Sheldon Durkey, Joseph Ricks, Nathaniel Evans, Daniel Downer, and Rufus Fish and his brother. She carried two of them while the others waded through the water with their arms around each other's necks and clinging to her skirts. Somehow they reached the opposite bank.

As night closed in, Mrs. Handy huddled in the

woods with the little brood she had rescued from certain death. One little fellow was so terrified by the experience that he never spoke again.

This mother did what few men would have dared to do—and what none could have accomplished. She was a woman. She was a mother.

It will take that kind of courage in our day, and it will take defiance of a power more destructive than an invading army, if the ideals of motherhood are to be protected. In our generation once again mothers will need to be heroines. They may well rescue their own children and future generations from another kind of invasion that even now moves into our settlements.

The *selflessness of a mother.* The influence of mothers and the power that develops within their children comes from the most ordinary of experiences in life. Children remember these "ordinary" experiences, which foster tender virtues that make men righteous and powerful. Let me illustrate.

I have heard President Marion G. Romney tell of his family fleeing northern Mexico before the armies of Pancho Villa. His mother, with seven little children and with all their worldly goods in one small trunk, crossed the Mexican border into Texas on a train laden with refugees. (Incidentally, another passenger on that train was young Camilla Eyring, later to be the wife of President Spencer W. Kimball.)

Later the father rejoined the Romney family.

There was a terrible struggle to get reestablished. He did whatever he could to take care of his family, and there were few extras in those difficult days. Almost never would there be an apple or some candy. When something special came along, Brother Romney remembers, "Mother never did want any."

That was sixty years ago or more, but he cannot mention the experience today without a catch in his throat as he recalls the sacrifices and selflessness of his mother.

The lessons of a mother. There is something about the ordinary, everyday influence of a mother that is more powerful than the spectacular events that capture the interest of the world. Let me tell you two lessons I learned from my mother.

Many years ago my parents lived in a very modest home in a small farming community. One morning my mother answered a knock at the door and was confronted there by a large, frightening-looking man who asked her for money.

She said, "We have no money." In that home there were several little children, but little money.

He pressed his demands, insisting that she give him some money. Finally he said, "I am hungry. I would like to get something to eat."

"Well," she said, "if that is the case, I can help you." So she hurried to the kitchen and fixed him a lunch. And I am sure it was the most modest of provisions.

17

She could tell as she handed him the lunch at the door that he was not pleased, but with little resistance he took it and left. She watched as he went down the lane through the gate and started up the road. He looked back but did not see her standing inside the door. Then, as he passed the fence line, he threw the lunch over the fence into the brush.

Now my mother was a little Danish woman, and she was angry. In that house there was nothing to waste, and she was incensed at the man's ingratitude.

The incident was forgotten until a week or two later when she answered another knock at the door. There stood a tall, raw-boned teenage boy who made an appeal in essentially the same words: "We need help. We are hungry. Could you give us some money? Could you give us some food?"

Somehow the image of the first man appeared in her mind and she said, "No." Then, excusing herself, she added, "I am sorry. I am busy. I cannot help you today. I just cannot help you." What she meant was, "I won't be taken in again."

The young man turned without protest and walked out the gate, as she stood looking after him.

It wasn't until he passed through the gate that she noticed the wagon, the father and mother, and the other youngsters. As the boy swung his long legs into the wagon, he looked back rather forlornly. Then the father shook the reins and the wagon went on down the road. She had hesitated just long enough so that she could not call them back.

From that experience she learned a lesson that she incorporated into her own life and that she imparted to her children. Fifty years afterwards there was still a hint of pain as she recalled the incident and stressed this moral: "Never fail to give that which you have to someone who is in need." This was a mother teaching her children in a most impressionable manner.

The second lesson, as is often the case, was taught by example. There are many women whose love extends beyond their own family. In elementary school I learned this great lesson.

In our school were several youngsters from a family not blessed with an attentive mother at home. During the school year they were afflicted with impetigo, a common disease of the skin that is now very easily cured. Because they were not bathed and because their clothing was not clean, the infection quickly spread across their bodies.

The principal asked my mother, who was the room mother for our class, to visit the home in the hope that she could encourage the type of care these children so badly needed. "The woman's touch," he said, "will be most helpful there." Although she responded to the request, she failed in her mission, for she found circumstances in that home pitiable.

Well do I remember the invitation to bring these little youngsters home from school with us. And, I remember, they were bathed; medication was applied to their little bodies; they were dressed in our clo-

20

thing; and in the early evening they were sent to their own home, to return the next day for the same treatment.

Night after night after night I remember my mother scrubbing endlessly with a bottle of disinfectant and then boiling clothing against the possibility that her own family might become infected. But her mother's heart would not turn them away, for these were little children, and they were suffering.

The love of a mother. Much of what I know that matters most, I have learned from my children and from their mother.

Some years ago my wife and I watched two of our little boys wrestling on the rug before the fireplace. As they reached that pitch—you know the one—where laughter turns to tears and play becomes a struggle, my wife and I agreed that something should be done. I worked a foot gently between them and lifted the older boy, then just four years of age, to a sitting position on the rug. I said, "Hey there, you monkey, you'd better settle down." He folded his arms and looked at us with surprising seriousness. His little-boy feelings had been hurt and he protested, "I not a monkey, Daddy. I a person."

How deeply we loved him. How much we wanted for him to be "a person," one of eternal worth, for "children are an heritage of the Lord." (Psalm 127:3.)

We shall not forget the tempering influence of

this lesson, one of the many lessons we learned from our children.

I love and respect the mother who gave these children to me. As they leave our "nest" they go into an uncertain world. They are fortified with a mother's love and example. She has prepared them, and they carry with them the memory of a happy home life. We have labored with great effort to give them that as an inheritance—the memory of a happy home life. It is the mother, more than any other, who makes that happy memory.

The gift of life and the mother love that attends it surely are among the supreme gifts of God. I know that the Lord loves mothers. He has said that not even the fall of a sparrow would escape His notice. How readily, then, will He bless those mothers who seek Him.

Their mother gave my children to me, and my mother gave me life. With reverence I say, as well we all might say, God bless, please bless, mothers.